In a Mirror...

James Percival

Published in 2024 by
GREEN CAT BOOKS
19 St Christopher's Way
Pride Park
Derby
DE24 8JY
www.green-cat.shop

Copyright © 2024 James Percival

All rights reserved.

ISBN: 978-1-913794-73-6

No part of this publication
may be reproduced in any form or by any
means without the prior written permission of
the publisher.

This book is sold subject to the conditions that
shall not, by way of trade or otherwise, be lent,
resold, hired out, or otherwise circulated without
the publisher's prior consent in any form of
binding other than that in which it is published
and without a similar condition including this
condition being imposed on the subsequent
purchaser.

DEDICATION

To my wife and long time friend Lesley and to my children, Rob and Rebekah.

CONTENTS

Acknowledgements	i
A Place to Reflect	2
Braveheart	4
Broken	6
Carried	8
Echoes by the Sea	10
Empty Place	14
Face Down	16
Face	18
Father and Son	20
Forever Yours	24
From a Distance	26
From the Darkness	30
From the Wreckage	34
Grateful	36
Great Heights	38
Images	42
In Simplicity	46

No Man's Land	50
November Dusk	52
Perception	54
Pierced Heart	58
Respect	60
Rhythm	62
Spectres	66
Summer Break	68
Sunrise	70
Thank You	74
The Child	76
The Fever	78
The Fight	82
The Guitarist	84
The Sea	88
To Love	92
Twilight	94
Vulnerable	96

Walking	98
Warmth	100
Who Cares	102
You Cannot Heal	104

ACKNOWLEDGEMENTS

Thanks go to my family for their belief in me. I would also thank the friends who have encouraged me to write these reflections down; their feedback has been invaluable. To publish these was not my initial aim nor the impetus behind the work; but there are many, both who have featured in the reflections and those whose feedback brought me to the point of believing they might be of use to others. Thank you for the shared journey.

In a Mirror...

A Place to Reflect

There are places for us all that may hold a special meaning – a place of sweet remembrance, of reconciliation, of new life...of deep peace; a place of resurrection? If we do not recognise such places, we need to go on our own pilgrimage to find them. And find them we will, but remembering too that the journey there may be significant in itself. New horizons beckon.
Buen Camino

IN A MIRROR…

Breathing space,
time out.
Fragrance instilled,
vision restored.
Erratic heartbeat
steadied by love.
Cradled in the
gentlest of arms.
Clarity of thought
and
purpose rekindled,
fanned by the wind of the Spirit.

Braveheart

Some journeys must be made alone, but there is something beautiful and synergistic about walking side by side with a loved one. The sense of comradeship and purpose is very strong, despite fallings-out, selfishness and stubborn pride. Learning to travel with others can be a lifelong commitment; but sadly, this seems to be increasingly hard to find. And struggle is ok ... may we see the return of the lost art of perseverance.

IN A MIRROR...

We struggle, you and I
side by side, against the flow.
I need your touch and I hope you need mine.
I will always stand by you, to turn
the anger away.

God meant us to be - to be us and
no-one else. Proud to be alive,
proud to be your friend.
We are what we are and
there is a place for us here – a heart
to be reached, a purpose to fulfil.

I stand to hold your hand,
hearts to beat as one.
Braveheart, you give me strength.
Let us fight to the end and
let the hurt go, for it has no place here.

Broken...

Suffering in any form is difficult to understand – what purpose does it serve?
We live in an imperfect world, a fallen world. Yet love only really proves itself in the place of suffering.
There is something enduringly true about suffering – that in some deep, strange way, it is redemptive and can be used to redeem others or even situations.

Broken heart;
tail end of deceit,
a disappointment,
love redundant.

Broken mind;
labour intensive,
overloaded impulse,
sparking in the dark...

Broken body;
disabled, frightened,
Vulnerable once again,
strength gone.

Broken spirit;
lost at sea,
hope fades,
a tear wells in the eye of God.

Bind my heart, heal my mind, restore my body, renew my spirit.
In doing these things, bring wholeness to others.

Carried

Life is complicated. For all of us, no matter what our circumstances are, there is a steady ebb and flow of the tides – of comings and goings, success and failure, peaks and deep valleys. The task is arduous and how is it that we survive? We need to accept the love and support of others as well as give it. Sometimes we can walk the path alone, buoyant and successful. But at others, we need each other – and we may have a new realisation of our need for God. To carry another is to be Christ-like. To be carried is difficult for some... and what is it like to be carried? We need to remember a parent carrying the struggling child and be comforted in the arms.

Alone, it seems, at times
a fight to be fought
against the odds;
Endless demands,
heights unobtainable
goals unreachable;
Dying embers, aglow,
weak beyond measure
until...

God's Spirit touches in
the gentlest of ways.

A hand held out;
'I'm with you',
Endless value placed upon me.
All that I'm worth
far exceeding expectation,
made possible through the prayer of faithful ones.

Carried by love

... and ready to carry...

Echoes by the Sea...

Giving God space is not easy. The world is full of 'white noise'... distractions, voices, shouts, moans... a cacophony! It's hard to sift the grain from the chaff, to distinguish the important from the trivial. So too with the spirit. To find a deeper peace and listen, we may need to create a space, or indeed find a place, where connection can be made. This might be described as a 'thin place', as the ancient Celts used to do. I live by the sea and the beach has provided such a place for me.

IN A MIRROR...

IN A MIRROR...

Lonely place I know so well,
calm waters shimmering with a bluey tinge
still reflecting the dying embers
of a crimson sunset.
Currents once beset with anger
now calm in the lingering embrace
of the evening sky.
A gentle breeze whispers my name
and turns my head to
a memory of this place and
echoes of His voice.

A meal shared here reminds me
once more that I hunger for the
Presence that restored me
despite the many failings of my life.

All I see now are the weathered remains of
a charcoal fire,
long extinguished by
the ebb and flow of life's tide.

Where do I go from here?
The face I can no longer see
has been replaced by the voice that calls
me still to a place beyond this one,
where, I do not know,

nor when…

But the truth I hold to is this; that He loved me once, despite
the fear and shame that nearly took me from His side.

'Follow me still...'

His voice refrains
and echoes once more through the shadowed
canyons
of my soul...

Empty Page

Life is tangled. What happens to us as we grow? Looking back at who we were can remind us in the complexity of life that we were once mercifully free of worry – or at least a consciousness of it. How do we regain that simple freedom to be ourselves. Maybe in the presence of a child... a loved one? We may realise that love has always held us ... and always will.

Empty page,
Empty heart,
restless spirit yearning deep
within... a daughter's love providing
hope, reason to live, clinging on.

O to be a child again!

Innocence lost, dreams betrayed...
How can I know fulfilment?
This truth is all is know
that I belong to the one who died.

Yearning to touch, to make whole.

'O love that will not let me go...

Face Down...

In the scramble for success and in the stampede of life, it's easy sometimes to feel down-trodden and disorientated. In the mud we can lose perspective and see only the darkness. Slipping off the duckboards into the mire...
We need to accept the helping hand of friends to lift us up to see the new horizon and to feel the sun again on our faces. And we, too, can be the one to lift others up and to hold steady the trembling hand.

IN A MIRROR...

Working, smiling, fevered activity;
forward and backward,
endless task, withering of intent
and strength that ebbs.

All that is strong, suddenly fragile
and falling under the gravity of guilt.
Disintegration, fissured emotion,
seething and escaping through
vents of despair.
Laid low, impotent
in the mud of life, face down,
coughing up clods of failure
mixed with the blood of passion.

Such love...
Holding my hand,
grip firm but gentle
lifting me up;
Fingers on my fallen chin,
raising my gaze to His, eyes met,
reassurance gained, strength
instilled.
Spirit of the One laid low,
breathing new life.

Face

Modern life is at breakneck speed. This inevitably leads to dehumanisation – life becomes two-dimensional and lacks depth. Communication is fraught with urgency and superficiality and it's often the way that we are on the receiving end of indifference. Will anyone listen? And does this affect us to the point of being this way with others? Is life becoming an endless stream of unrealistic demands on our time?

The closeness of God allows us to find a better way to find a life of richer relationships. We may give more space to others and ourselves become stronger to face the demands made on us.

IN A MIRROR…

Deadlines pressing,
hard, simmering edges;
Hissing panic,
shaking with fear.
Half-hearted smile; measured
response; cold, lifeless,
uncertain – confidence knocked,
perfection misfired, tainted.
Strained emotion, stretched
to breaking

        Disappointed, character flaw,
expectation unrealistic…
Human response that damages…

Yet all is well…

I face all things with you.

Thank you for taking me as I am.

Father and Son

Trying to please parents is an impossible task and best left alone. There is often little we can do to stave off the inevitable sigh of disappointment. Yet surely the fault lies somewhat with the parent – are expectations unrealistic... do parents just want to recreate versions of themselves? Surely what we must hope for our children is a fulfilment of potential and self respect - and a potential they recognise and see for themselves. When our children struggle, we need to be there to support from the sidelines and cheer them over the line.

IN A MIRROR...

IN A MIRROR...

I saw myself play
on the pitch today...
Tired limbs,
an inward drive, needing
to succeed, needing
to please.

But out of place, contorted
shapes; grating feeling
a frustration within –
Displeased with self and yet
are others to blame?
Out of position, defence or attack...
Who knows?
A knock to the knee
and a hurting, limp.

Yet does it matter where he plays,
as long as he knows
his place and his ordained role?

IN A MIRROR…

I stood there as a father stands,
proud to view his son
with all his effort and struggle.
I loved him as he was and
cared not should he succeed or fail,
save for his self-respect.

I am proud of you as you stand,
for you are never a failure to me.

Forever Yours

'Beauty is in the eye of the beholder'. If this is true, then God must see us differently than we see ourselves or even maybe, as others see us. His deep love for us is almost impossible to grasp this side of the grave. We get mere glimpses – a look, a glance, a smile maybe? The rest is up to faith.
And the cost of the passion? Why is suffering so caught up with redemption?
We must turn this love outwards that others, too, may see the truth. Faith and hope join hands to open the door to the discovery of true love.

IN A MIRROR…

A hand to hold,
I feel your strength, yet
hard to believe the weight of passion;
My freedom, what cost?
I have been slow to learn
but learn I have,
recognising love in pain.

I begin to see the hurt in others.
Wary, frightened eyes that hide
clenched fists within.

A reluctance to touch or be touched
A tug from the reins of constraint.

Lord, may they know your touch
In mine; your voice in softened tones.

Don't let them hurt.

Peace will come…

From a Distance...

Many of us find change difficult, whether we bring it about ourselves or change 'happens' to us, leaving us feeling vulnerable and without familiar reference points. It's these times of imposed change that we may find the hardest to handle. We may see ourselves in this situation at the moment. It is important that we see this time as transient – yes, the period of change may seem to go on for a long time, yet in the great scheme of the tangle of life, all things pass and a new resolution emerges. We need to be firm in our hope that God holds all things, including us.

IN A MIRROR…

IN A MIRROR...

What lies in the distance is hazy, unclear,
shadowed;

FORMLESS

What is near, immediate is clear, calm and at
peace –

Beautiful, changing, yes, but in its time.
I am in the here and now...

Yesterday was the past,
Tomorrow is the future,
Today is God's gift to us, that's why it's called
the 'present'...

Take hold this gift.
Be myself.
What will emerge will be beautiful,
formed in the chrysalis of darkness,
cramped and hurting.
A chink of light offers
the possibility of hope.

IN A MIRROR...

What lies in the distance
will become eventually
what is near – no longer hazy, unclear, shadowed but
clear, calm and at peace – beautiful.

Let God be the one to take me there...

From the Darkness

We often talk of the journey from the light into a dark place where we lose our way. There are indeed many things that lure us there and before we know it, we find ourselves in the middle of a dark labyrinth where all is disfigured and confusing. Yet the light beckons us too and wooes us with the promise of hope and peace. We must look to the light and be steadfast to find our way home and turn our backs on the darkness.

IN A MIRROR...

IN A MIRROR...

The darkness sneers
as if to bring me down;
Each step now a laboured task,
unsure of the way ahead and
the steps that lead me home.

Stumbling becomes a common thing,
despite my arms outstretched
to guide me and protect
me from the fall;
Burdens heavy under the furrowed brow
of the purveyor of gloom.
Songs of pain that sound
hollow in the stillness of the night.

Yet a flicker comes, at least at first...

then grows to pierce the darkest glade
with its powerful ray.
My head is lifted and
my eyes strain to see its form.
So I walk on to find the source,
find the nature of the warmth.

The power of darkness begins
to wane and lose its grip upon my soul...
The path before me shimmers
like a steely thread that leads me on.

The light beckons and
the dawn brings with it
a gentle smile... a look
from the face of one
who has lived a life of beauty
and which calls me to a better way...
Where souls might journey
and find their peace at last.

The Light shines in the darkness, but
the darkness has never overcome it.

From the Wreckage…

Life can seem, at times, like being in a crucible. Do we then just grin and bear the searing heat and sense of falling apart, or see ahead to a time when we hold the precious, refined product in our hands? Scars remain, but a stronger, more determined spirit? And our own scars can be transformed into reminders of pain, but not slaves to them. And new love blossoms and colours return…

IN A MIRROR...

Limp and lifeless,
skin burnt and blackened
by life's bitter caress...
encased in dreams that have
long since died;
Semi-conscious of darkened rooms that
have no life within.

Blood pumping, contaminated
With every broken dream
that aspires to capture me,
yet drops to lie
shattered on the ground of this life...

Still, from the fire I have
survived to tell the tale
of love that goes deeper than me
and grants the grace
to hold fast the truth
that I am me, and grateful too....

Grant me rest, that these wounds
may heal and not leave me disfigured,
but prone to love as you do.

Grateful

Connecting with the elements recolours our world. The feel of the wind, the rage of the sea, the mist settling in the corries on a mountain side. In all the confusion and pain, the earth sets us on a course to a deep recognition that we are intimately linked with something ancient; something deep and rooted in the passage of time. Then we smile on the clifftop as we see the stars. We are very little... but valued none-the-less.

IN A MIRROR...

Breeze blowing
fresh on the face,
A cooling balm to the soul.
Refreshing inside,
purging hurt and fear.
Beautiful colours, hues and
tones untold.
Nodding in agreement,
dancing with joy...
held in the arms of the Designer, cherished.
Provision made and needs tended, lovingly.

Calm inside, at last.
A glimpse through His eyes...
How I am loved.
May the vision never go.

Grateful heart.

Great Heights

Jumping from a plane, even with a parachute attached, is frightening. The safety of the plane gives way to the onset of panic as you edge closer to the door. When you finally jump, the exhilaration sucks your breath away. Then, all goes quiet and it seems that you are floating, seeing the world as never before.
The earth below suddenly looms big – and, although the 'chute has opened, will I make it? Still sometimes we hit the ground at speed...

IN A MIRROR…

IN A MIRROR…

Flying high above the world,
horizon blue with haze
and a wind that takes my breath away.
Sitting on the edge of safety,
held by someone I do not know…

A gentle rocking
gives way to a tumble
into the vast unknown.

Everything blurs in that spiral fall –
All senses out of their depth,
Not even time to breathe.
With one look,
the world is transformed.
Slow motion and floating on an unknown sea…
Knowing a peaceful caress,
the freedom to fall, exposing
a view 'til now unseen.

IN A MIRROR…

Still, the earth looms at an alarming pace,
cords cut, all alone
once again –
Hitting the ground at speed,
spread-eagled in despair -
tasting mud
and spitting stones.

Colours blur,
but give rise to the land once again,
rich and green.

Images

Depression is insidious. It lurks in the shadows and distracts from the path. Before you know it, it instils its presence in your being and lays you low. Confusion blurs the picture as the spirit within us tries to grapple with the unknown and unfamiliar intrusion – and not necessarily accompanied with the 'feeling' of depression; rather, concentration is a struggle, life becomes breathless and moving as if you wade through treacle and drive with the brakes on. Yet these are just the first skirmishes in a series that, with love, support and the simple feat of putting one foot in front of the other, will end in peace... and a more complete human being.

IN A MIRROR…

IN A MIRROR...

Faded tones,
a mirror image
of a troubled soul,
swirling mist of
a myriad of feelings; Confused,
enshrouded in fear.

Darkness surrounded by light,
engulfed in love;
warm tears, soft with the
gentlest of touches.

Unreal, out of the body,
gazing at familiar ones
wanting to hold, yet fearing touch...

And oblivion, what of you?
Your lure is strong, I can see your shadow;
An easy option, 'I won't be missed...'

Where will I go?
Part of me is damaged within;
Faded edges, torn emotion,
something delicate has broken,
a thousand pieces, laid out.

I have lost myself.

Held by loving hands
Shaped for the purpose
of love.

This is a place of suffering...

The darkness is real,
Yet still only a passage in time...

... that ushers in contentment and a brighter
day.

In Simplicity...

Living in the world today can seem very complicated, often unnecessarily so; relationships, demands, time pressures, workload... even how we buy food and get resources – all topped with the cacophony of mass communication.
How do we 'unclutter'? When seen at a very basic level, life is, in fact, incredibly simple. There are very few things we actually need to survive and live well. This is also true at a spiritual level. Surely even main religious and theological issues have become far too complicated. We can no longer see the simple truths for the wall of 'words' that hems us in on all sides.

IN A MIRROR...

IN A MIRROR...

In simplicity...
You came
to a cold, damp place,
feeling the touch of the world you had made.

In simplicity...
You grew
toward a calling,
Presence of God amongst the people.

In simplicity...
You gave
all things
to a race broken and divided, lost.

In simplicity...
You died,
life draining away
and given to bring us home.

In simplicity..
You returned
alive, with a smile
caressing our fears away to a distant place.

In simplicity..
I give
myself to you.
Hold me close as we journey together in this life.

Bring me home...

No Man's Land

Sometimes the darkness is overpowering and the battle seems lost. Life can suck all the strength from within us. We are left floundering and disorientated amid the noise. If we retreat or attack – there is no certainty of success, for we are vulnerable whatever direction we go in. We may just have to wait ... and ride out the storm and grapple with the perennial question: 'Will I make it?'

IN A MIRROR...

Neither here nor there

For or against,
won or lost.
Groping, clawing at the earth,
determined to survive,
yet impotent.
At the mercy of fate.
Conscious of rhythm,
a thudding, irregular pulse
Breathless despair;
Will I make it?

Wounded, I make it
home,
once again to face the sun
and sense the peace.

November Dusk

In the overall tapestry of our lives, we may never have the opportunity to stand back and see the picture as a whole. In the midst of life, as the threads weave and twist, we see mere fragments and we struggle to see purpose and design; perhaps it is in the eyes of others that we find ourselves and discover more fully our place in the overall design?

IN A MIRROR...

In silence images clear,
wrought in coldness,
stark against the pastel sky.

Angular, jagged, yet at peace – a silence
within, profound, bringing memories
of distant days, faded and pale...

The threads that bind together the tapestry
display an image of what was meant to be...
fate or in our hands these threads?

And in death, the picture complete,
gathered themes and honed pain
to forge the final image pleasing
to the Father's eye, the likeness
of His Son.

Why this way?

Are there no others?

The way of suffering is clear...
but brings life to all who walk its
stark reality, the image complete.

Perception

It can be very difficult to change a poor self-image. It may take lots of time; reflection, discussion, soul- searching... to be honest with ourselves can be an uphill struggle. And listening to the platitudes and encouragement from others can fall on deaf ears. All of us have an inner beauty, no matter what life has obscured and damaged. Self-perception can be cruelly inaccurate.

Helping people to see their worth is what it means to truly love; the truth may yet be found.

IN A MIRROR...

IN A MIRROR...

A tense moment,
sickly smile, thoughts perspiring to
droplets on a furrowed brow,
coalescing to a trickle of self-doubt.
To breathe, a laboured task,
suddenly aware of pulse,
colour drained, spiralling to earth, wasted.

Yet glad anticipation, keen to go, trusting
eyes and minds;
Known by them and trusted too.
Mistakes made, but to no avail –
Nothing undone, damaged, curtailed
by the grace of his presence.

The smile that says, 'why do you
see yourself thus?
How you perceive and
are perceived are different entities,
worlds apart...'

I know it grates and hurts inside,
but you must learn to see the difference...
The turmoil inside is rarely seen,
The outward expression translated into
something loving and meaningful by my love.

It isn't you they see...
I stand with you always, perceived or not.

Pierced Heart

No-one is immune to pain. It is something with which we all grapple, fight against and experience in time; it seems destructive and often redundant. Although we are at its mercy and can seemingly do little to wriggle from its grip, maybe there is some way to redeem it. Indeed, it is pain that warns, that sometimes guides and even saves us. In the anger of the moment when it strikes, however strong or bitter, breathe a little and take the blow. Hope paints the colours of a better day and pain endured gives rise to strength.

IN A MIRROR...

 Life pulls its bow taut
and aims at the vulnerability of the heart.

Swift the arrow flies
and pierces the defences with ease.

Straight to the centre
of all that is me...

Heart nailed to an
ancient beam, too painful to withdraw.

Lifelessness stalks my limbs;
Senses dim...

The kind platitudes of life
no use to me now.

Pain wells to the surface,
river swollen to bursting.

Hope fades... strength fails;
Engulfed in a haze of weariness.

Is there a balm for this wound?
Who will break the shaft in two
and relieve its cruel intent?

Respect

The early parts of the journey can be particularly bewildering. So much can happen 'to' us and it seems we are too often victims of another's neglect. We are plagued by naivety, and coping strategies are weak; we are vulnerable. We can look back and feel a sense of failure; yet decisions made were the best we could make at the time and we need to be gentle with ourselves. Instead of calling ourselves foolish, we need to have a realistic picture of who we were, and are, and by whom we are loved.

Love for ourselves is necessary as we seek to truly love others. This begins with self-respect...

IN A MIRROR...

Respect is what I give you
truly and honestly.
You hold on to
all that you know to be true.

And what is true?

God's love for me
and my love for you;
That is true.
You command respect and
I stand and admire
all that you are
and all that you have allowed to be achieved...

Well done.

Rhythm

Connectedness is a phrase much talked about today. More are realising the need to break free from the overload of the tuneless and hopeless dirge that seems to seek to engulf us day to day. Somehow in our culture we have become dull in our hearing to the basic rhythm of life that has been here from the beginning. We need to stop and learn to listen... and to look at the whole of nature and rediscover meaning and our place in this beautiful world.

IN A MIRROR...

IN A MIRROR...

Random thoughts in
a random world,
out of place and out of sync.
Sounds blare from the trumpets of trivia
... songs that have no beginning
and may have no end.
No meaning, lost in tangles
of weeds and nameless thorns.
The wind blows, from where
no-one knows;
Blown this way and that with
no anchor to steady the
heart and calm the mind.

Yet when all is stripped
and calm,
when we listen instead of speak
and turn the volume down,
we can hear the heart beat again
and find comfort in its steady pulse,
overlaid by a rhythm from
ancient times.
Then other rhythms come to mind:
The sea has her tides,
The Moon its phases,
The Earth its cycle of life.

IN A MIRROR…

Let me walk once again to the beat
of this ancient song and
its healing rhythms.

Spectres

Walking at night in an unknown place is only made worse by the half-light diffused by mist. Easy to get lost in and very disorientating. What were familiar objects become disfigured into demons and things of the imagination; fear rises from the darkness of the earth.
So, too, with our spirits... fear grips and darkness pervades to bring us to the place of the dark night of the soul. A place of confusion, of lostness. But a place we have to know to understand the light of redemption.

IN A MIRROR...

Unsure, wayward, lost.
Turbulent mist, swirling in shadowed spectres,
Wide-eyed, anxious; where do I go?
Reaching out, trying to hold on
to what I know to be true.
Fear, gripping a strangle-hold
on the rhythm of life,
stumbled, clumsy and confused.

Yet the faithfulness of the hurt one,
a touch of love from ancient wood,
a smile of reassurance from one
who has known fear and pain.
A hug that squeezes out tension.
I am loved by the Faithful One and touched by an indirect route of love.

Unexpected...

But yet He came to rescue me from fear.

Summer Break

The life – work balance is often talked about. It is an easy concept to grasp, but very hard to live it out day to day. Before we know it, life has once again brought us to a place of disillusionment and weariness. It's important to remain active in the pursuit of recreation, not for its own sake, but for the sake of our overall well-being and rounded view of life. It is almost a self-discipline!

IN A MIRROR...

An ocean of time
revealing soft sands to the touch.
Jewelled days and gentle breeze
sifting the mind of dark
seedlings that land in the soil of doubt.

Gentle pause in the
frantic struggle;
A sure repose and stilling of the heart,
beautiful colours, opening the eyes
and dazzling the senses; quiet laughter...
Lost in time, no deadlines to meet.
Holding hands, safe in the hands that hold us
both.

Peace breathed deeply, allowing the soul
contact with vibrant air, invigorating...
The soul breathes freely again,
unrestrained, smiling;

The balm of this earth softly applied to the
wounds that mar the image...

Tainted, but unspoilt, beautiful.

Sunrise

It's no wonder that darkness holds the monopoly on the symbolism of fear. Nothing seems real, all seems vague, unfamiliar with dark shadows that loom to create unknown demons. And what is 'the dark night of the soul'? We toss and turn awaiting the end of the gloom... and time drags. In the small hours, we hold on to hope... and welcome the sunrise.

IN A MIRROR…

IN A MIRROR...

I know the darkness of abandonment.
I know the frailty of time.
I know the decisions that lead to a
dead-end of emotion...

Of loss that taunts in
accusing whispers of doubt;
echoes of voices,
images that rise and fall,

        come and go,
        sharpen and fade.

Tears that fall
and splash in the pool of remembrance,
sending out ripples of consciousness.

In the confusion,
let grace have its way;
Let its gentle hand
soothe and touch
the very place of pain.

Still my soul.
Cool the fever of restlessness,
hold my hand.
Bring me gently to the place of contentment

..................and to a swift sunrise.....

Thank You

We carry perhaps many burdens from past experiences. Some hurts can be prone to fester due to lack of air and sun. Recognising pain is important and it's a good thing when hurts come out into the light to be shrivelled and rendered less painful. Gratitude comes and a sense of release follows. We do not need to be held by pain; let redemption take its course.

IN A MIRROR...

Thank you for

Soothing refreshment to my soul
wrought in sunshine
and the warmth of a smile,
fashioned in the heat of anger.
Molten feeling, bubbling on the
hot stones of sub-conscious pain.
Yet a release, a break from the mould,
an un-chaining.

Freedom to be me,
loved for who I am
and not what I aspire to be.

The Child

It's easy to blame our past for our actions in the present. We must resist the temptation to do this because we all need to take responsibility for what we do and say. All are damaged and we must seek to redeem the pain and create something of beauty from the wreckage.

IN A MIRROR...

Quiet memories of
early days – summer sun and carefree hours, often
alone.
Blonde hair and red shoes, building places of
refuge from the looming world.
Birdsong on the breeze and leaves that
rustle; delicate blossoms reflecting a delicate soul.

Then life intrudes and presents its
poison, albeit insidious at first.
The looks that bode well hide a deeper
truth – that all is not well.
Deception injected into my veins, the loss of trust
like a dagger to the heart.
Will the pain inflicted cripple me
for life, despite the love and
care from those I hold dear?
Will the little boy survive
 or is he crushed
and broken like a reed?

Only the one who has suffered too will know.

Yet I cannot blame the past for the
way I treat the world.
I am responsible to the call of love
and it is love that will save me still.

The Fever...

Sometimes we find ourselves in unknown territory and seemingly alone. Our ailments are played out on the loudspeakers of fear with no-one to listen but ourselves. When will the fever break?
All things pass and we are never truly alone. We must hold on to the ones we love and mop their brows in whatever ways we can. The sea will not always be angry. One day it will calm and return gracefully on a new tide.

IN A MIRROR…

IN A MIRROR...

 Bleary-eyed, I
stagger through the day;
body made of lead,
on all fours – victim
of my own determination.

Up and down, clear
then dull, bright then dark.

Breathing laboured
and a pulse that
strikes upon the anvil;
sparks fly
and cover the floor.
Imprisoned, it seems,
for now at least –
Dark shafts where
there is no light.

Hold me still
and let me rest with you…

IN A MIRROR...

May I see you in the new every day;
in the smallest of things and in
the smiling faces and
words of loved ones.

...and in the crashing of the sea.

The tide will turn....

The Fight

To give unselfishly is the call of the Christian. Yet, if this is all we do, then we will be in danger of losing the ability to receive and forget the gentle touch of grace. Indeed, not just forgetting what grace feels like, but in its final form, being unable to recognise it at all. There can be a perverse and unhealthy fascination with 'doing' things for others in isolation.

If we are to give, then we must also learn to receive.

IN A MIRROR...

Moulded and shaped
in the furnace of life,
responding to pressures untold;
Fight side-by-side
although, so often it seems, I
spurn the aid – forget the strength.
Sweat and toil 'til every last foe
is laid low, vanquished.

Yet there is nothing left and a
gentle smile says it all:

'Why did you did you not ask for help?'

The Father stroking the brow
of His child – heart warmed and
smiling spirit, raised.

'Am I loved as much?'

The Guitarist

Teaching and working with children is a privilege. Yet it is always hard to know to what extent you have 'reached' a child. It is easy to just feel the pressures, running around, complying with demands. It is very hard to take stock and measure 'success', whatever that is.
It is warming to meet some ex-pupils, sometimes in the most unexpected places and realise that a life has been touched and that they are doing well.

IN A MIRROR…

IN A MIRROR...

Meaningful day, busy
with many tasks,
but a break from the routine
to view the sun
in a different light.

Warm face, disfigured past
haunted by spectres of failure –
A task undone, a child
not reached, impatience rife
in a world of pressured existence.

'Well done, but what else do you
have to give?'
Everything is no longer enough...

But in that place, I recognised a face
beknown to me – familiar, essentially
the boy I knew – frail still and shy.
Greeting warm, blushed memory,
a child once in my care.
I've not forgotten the gentle crossing of
paths – and still I hear music
in his voice, clear notes in life's tangled melody.
His smile has warmed my heart,
a life touched by grace;
perhaps it was worth the struggle after all...?

IN A MIRROR...

It was the guitarist.

The Sea

Human ears are tuned to the spoken word and so often the spoken language of nature is blotted out or simply unrecognised. Somehow over time, we have lost the art of listening to the beautiful melodies from which we have become unfamiliar and whose rhythm we no longer dance to. To stare at and listen to the sea in all its moods gives opportunity to the ancient language to be spoken again – hopefully we can learn to hear its prophetic message once more?

IN A MIRROR…

IN A MIRROR...

It comes and goes,
dances and lies still.
It rises and falls,
its deep heart pulsing from depths below.

No one can see her face to face,
just expressions of mood that moves
silently towards the shore – touching souls
and drawing patterns on the sand.

Strong... silent, yet crashing sometimes with an ugly face
when anger flows through and finds its
way, dissipated by the rocks and smashing the strongest of wills;
Power and gentleness oft combine
to lay waste the strongholds of man.

Where do you come from?

And where do you go?

IN A MIRROR...

Something ancient and permanent dwells here -
Something that connects us
with the first breath of life
and the continuing story of this coated rock.

Will you take me home or just offer the sure
rhythm of life that lulls me to sleep at night?

Teach me to be still and listen to your
hidden voice; teach me of the ancient ways.

Let me learn the language of the sea
so I, too, can know the truths of a bigger,
yet unseen world.

To Love...

Life is about relationship and this is itself rooted in both giving and receiving, active and passive. One-way traffic is always frustrating, no matter from which angle you come. We need to embrace the flow of life, both away from us and towards us. It is a joy to give out, but also a joy to receive the love of others.

To understand,
To be understood
Is the joy of life.

To challenge,
To be challenged
Is the battle of life.

To find,
To be found
Is the journey of life.

To hold,
To be held
Is the wonder of life.

To know,
To be known
Is the intimacy of life.

To love,
To be loved
Is the essence of life.

Twilight

Life is tiring. We need to find ways to recuperate and rest; not always easy. Even in relative quiet, we can find that when sleep comes, we can still be troubled by some subconscious and unresolved issue. Dreams come, swirl and dance and leave us mystified when we awake. Our spirits cry out to be in that place of peace... where we can be ourselves and be true to ourselves.

IN A MIRROR...

Tired, the eyes protest
and close
to block the light.

Peace in the darkness...
or just a world held
at bay for a short while?

Yet the shadows roam,
gradually taking the ragged
shape of awkward memories.

Hands stretch to ward
them off, as if pushing
could flout the disassembled form!

Opening the eyes once more
to the polychrome
layers of life comes as some relief.

No longer shadowed
But life in all its
fullness now described.

Vulnerable

*To become vulnerable to another human being is the only true path to selfless loving. This presents real risk to the individual; indeed the risk of being 'wounded' (**vulnus** in Latin, 'wound') is high. True loving is costly... it's certainly not one way traffic, expecting to be loved all the time, but loving outwards. Vulnerability takes loving from the passive to the active.*
Yet in vulnerability we find our true selves... and a lasting, although costly peace, comes.

IN A MIRROR…

Exposed, face to face,
the stark reality of life
stretching out its long
fingers of uncertainty;
Touching the chords
of doubt that jangle
the dull notes of dissonance.

Cold, I hide my face.

The wind, whose icy breath
seeks to take mine away,
speaks a muted
language to my soul.
Shivers of fear betray
the tension within;
All is stripped away,
nowhere left to hide…

Yet, warmth pervades,
knowledge of me that runs deep
to stay the mind and shield my face,
protected by eternal purpose.

Shining through the darkness of time…

    Illuminating the vulnerability of love.

Walking

When a child is growing and finding their feet, is it always wise to pick the child up when the going gets tough? The knee-jerk of the parent is to do so, but wisdom says that if this happened every time a stumble came, the child would never learn to stand strong by themselves. A good, discerning parent knows when to intervene and when not to. Sometimes we need to stand strong.

On the quiet sands,
Walking an unsteady path
feeling the weight of sorrow's burden,
needing to be carried and yet not so…

He sometimes does not carry, for there is only
one set of footprints for sure.

Yet he stands… shadowing.

He knows the pain.

'I've known the same…'

Warmth

There is a lot to be said for modern technology and the subsequent social media epidemic. Instant responses come thick and fast and what matters, we can say what we like, where we like and not really bother with what others say?
But what is really becoming of human relationships... is there not a price to pay? There will never be any replacement for true contact – alive and vibrant, dangerous even; but we must never give up on the briefest of smiles, the look in the eye... or on the warmth of a touch.

Indifferent glance
closed ears, taking nothing in.
Shoulder turned;
invisible, ghostly presence.
walk right through...

Pushing aside
Ulterior motives,
Hidden agendas,
Sickly smile,
Eyeless contact.

Hello... goodbye.

Enough said.

Warmth... where have you gone?

Who cares?

It is a world divided. Those who give and those who take. Inevitably, we are a mixture of the two. For those who give more than they receive, who is there for them? The danger with giving out constantly is emotional and spiritual burnout. There must be a balance; but how do we achieve it?

IN A MIRROR...

Who cares for the carer?
Who shepherds the shepherd?
Who protects the protector?
Who holds the holder?
Who weeps for the weeper?
Who heals the healer?
Who saves the saviour?
Who comforts the comforter?
Who blesses the blesser?
Who teaches the teacher?

You Cannot Heal

How can we realistically and authentically walk alongside those who suffer? How, too, can we empathise with pain if we ourselves have not really felt its barbed sting? Kind platitudes are not enough. We must learn to learn from our own pain; to turn despair to hope and darkness into light. The great paradoxes of Christ's teaching help us to see that suffering is never redundant. This is equally true if we are to share our faith with any meaning. The only message that people really respond to is one that is lived and where love is real.

IN A MIRROR...

You cannot heal a heart
with one that has not been pierced.

You cannot see the truth
with eyes that have not wept.

You cannot touch a soul
with one that has not known the darkness of the night.

You cannot mop a brow
with a cloth that has not bandaged a wound.

You cannot hold a hand
with one not shaped by love.

You cannot carry a burden
with a back not already broken with load.

You cannot rise
unless you fall.

You cannot see
unless you're blind.

You cannot hold unless you let go.

You cannot live unless you die.

ABOUT THE AUTHOR

James Percival is a retired Primary School teacher with a background in medical pathology, having gained qualifications in microbiology. He has a heart for the protection of the Earth and loves to journey; not just in the physical sense, but alongside others in the passage of life.

For more information about our books and services, please visit

www.green-cat.shop

www.ingramcontent.com/pod-product-compliance
Lightning Source LLC
LaVergne TN
LVHW011210080426
835508LV00007B/710